Original title:
The Walls of Comfort

Copyright © 2025 Creative Arts Management OÜ
All rights reserved.

Author: Franklin Stone
ISBN HARDBACK: 978-1-80587-060-9
ISBN PAPERBACK: 978-1-80587-530-7

Tranquility's Nest

In my cozy nook, I seek to hide,
With snacks stacked high, a feast inside.
Socks unmatched, but who will care?
I sit and grin in my comfy chair.

The phone's on silent, let it ring,
Who needs the world? I'm doing my thing.
Pajamas all day, oh what a sight,
Snuggled in cushions, feeling just right.

My pet's the king, lounges with pride,
He judges me well as I gobble and glide.
Remote control's my trusty sword,
In the battle of boredom, I swing it forward.

So here I dwell, in this bubble of cheer,
With laughter and snacks, no worries near.
The outside chaos can wait in line,
In this world of comfort, everything's fine!

Secured Spaces

In my bubble, I hide away,
With socks that don't match in bright display.
A fortress of snacks, my loyal pets,
Dancing to tunes, no room for regrets.

The couch is my throne, a sight to behold,
Worn out and comfy, as stories unfold.
Pajamas my armor, I battle the day,
In this snug retreat, I laugh and I play.

Lullabies Behind Closed Doors

In pajamas I prance, it's quite the affair,
With mismatched slippers, who really would care?
The refrigerator hums a sweet serenade,
As I sip my juice, a grand escapade.

Tick-tock goes the clock, it's time for a snack,
With cookies and chips, there's no need to pack.
Under covers, I find my own tune,
While the cat makes a mess, dancing 'round like a loony.

Embracing the Known

My favorite show is the highlight today,
With chips on my lap, who wants to play?
The dog steals my sandwich, but I won't complain,
In this joyful chaos, there's nothing to feign.

Walls made of laughter, support and surprise,
With friends on my screen, oh how time flies!
We giggle and snort, in our cozy domain,
Every silly moment, a sweetest refrain.

A Fortress of Tranquil Feelings

In a den of delight, I cocoon myself tight,
With odd little treasures that give me sheer fright.
Puzzles half-finished lie scattered about,
While I juggle my socks, there's no need for doubt.

A duster my weapon, against dust I will fight,
As I sneak in a nap, just to feel right.
In this haven of giggles, I'm queen of my fate,
With laughter my ruler, I'll never be late.

Soft Borders of Belonging

In pajamas we dance, oh what a sight,
Tripping on slippers in the soft moonlight.
Sarcastic remarks from the cushions we throw,
In this silly circus, the laughter will grow.

Sneaky snack raids in the midnight hour,
Pillow forts rising, we'll claim our power.
Cranes of chaos in our cozy domain,
Each giggle a leaf on our joy-filled chain.

Serenity's Embrace

Cozy in chaos, a blanket brigade,
Sipping on cocoa as the mess is made.
The cat's on the keyboard, typing a song,
Whiskers in harmony; feel free to join along.

Loud movie nights with popcorn galore,
Flickering shadows dance on the floor.
Each moment a treasure, so light and free,
With friends in our bubble, just silly as can be.

Guarded Hearts and Hidden Halls

Hidden away like a sock's missing mate,
In our trusty fortress, we secretly skate.
Banana peels scattered, our laughter breaks free,
Pretending we're spies as we snack on our brie.

Shhh! The giggles hide behind closet doors,
While the cat takes the throne and gracefully snores.
With whispers of secrets and a few playful barks,
We rule our domain, leaving memorable marks.

Cuddled in Fragile Fortresses

Fortified laughter in a pillow-enclosed space,
Squeaky voices join in a peculiar race.
Plastic swords wielded, a battle for pride,
In our fragile fortresses, we take every stride.

Beneath the bedding, where silliness reigns,
Tickle fights breaking down all the chains.
Each chuckle like echoes, all worries depart,
In this hilarious haven, we craft every heart.

Refuge of Dreams

In pajamas I roam, a king in my lair,
Snacking on chips, without a single care.
Couch is my throne, remote in my hand,
A kingdom of comfort, oh isn't it grand!

My cat is the jester, in droopy repose,
Chasing her tail, as only she knows.
With Netflix as court, we binge every night,
In this refuge of dreams, everything's right.

Hedges of Harmony

My living room's like a park of delight,
With cushions and blankets piled high to the height.
The dogs are the guards, they bark at the door,
While squirrels in the yard plot for crumbs on the floor.

The scent of fresh popcorn fills up the air,
As laughter erupts—oh, how we do flare!
Neighbors all ponder, what fun can we share?
In hedges of harmony, no worries or care.

Pillars of Peace

The fridge is a fortress, stocked wide and full,
Ice cream a treasure, oh my what a pull!
I sit on my throne, a snack in each hand,
In this place of laughter, I feel so grand.

On sunny days, I nap in the sun,
Chasing the bees—this life is such fun!
With my blanket as shield, and dreams in my fold,
Pillars of peace, oh how they uphold.

Nurtured by Familiar Surroundings

In my cozy cocoon, nothing can go wrong,
With biscuits and tea, I hum my strange song.
The laundry's a mountain, I call it my art,
As clutter and chaos dance heart to heart.

Each room tells a tale, full of quirks and cheer,
With mismatched socks hiding, they share my dear fear.
Yet amidst all this madness, I grin ear to ear,
Nurtured by familiar, I hold it all dear.

Sanctuary of Shadows

In corners where dust bunnies play,
I sit on my throne, it's laundry day.
The couch tells secrets, the fridge sings too,
In my fort of cushions, I've got the view.

The cat is my guard, a fierce little queen,
She keeps watch for snacks and the occasional bean.
Though my kingdom's a mess, it feels like a dream,
And my laughter echoes, quite silly it seems.

Embracing the Echoes

The walls have ears, they hear my song,
I dance in my PJs, it feels so wrong!
Chasing the vacuum, I trip on a sock,
Yet, in this odd groove, I feel like a rock.

With echoes of giggles bouncing around,
I pull out the snacks; it's a fiesta profound!
Beneath all the chaos, a sweet joy I find,
In this wild serenade, I'm happily blind.

Safe Haven's Whisper

I built a retreat with pizza and fries,
Sweet chocolate rivers, oh what a surprise!
The walls are my allies, no judgment or frown,
In this cozy cocoon, I wear my crown.

The plants have opinions, the lamp nods along,
When I sing in the shower, I'm the star of the song.
A bubble of laughter, where giggles collide,
In my fortress of fun, I take silly pride.

Within the Fortress of Solitude

My fortress is packed with old board game loot,
Where I scheme with the cat; we're so astute.
Each snack is a treasure I hoard and I share,
With crumbs on my face, I don't have a care.

The dog brings the drama, a diva in fur,
We plot our escape, a quick neighborhood tour.
Through giggles and howls, my heart sings with glee,
In this silly stronghold, I'm perfectly free.

Greetings from the Enclave.

In a cocoon where snuggles reign,
A lazy sofa, a minor pain.
The fridge hums a tune so sweet,
In this hideaway, I never greet.

Chips and salsa dance around,
In secret corners, joy is found.
Pajamas are the fashion here,
Who needs the world? Nothing to fear.

Safe Havens Whisper

Blankets piled like towering peaks,
Where the cat plots and softly sneaks.
I sip my drink, while time does slow,
This fortress guards me from the flow.

Walls of snacks, my tasty moat,
A snack attack? Just grab a tote.
Netflix plays my silent friend,
In this kingdom, boredom won't descend.

Embracing Solitude's Embrace

Alone with my thoughts, a quirky dance,
In stillness, I take my silly stance.
The dust bunnies cheer, they know my name,
Reigning solo, it's a joyous game.

With mismatched socks and hair askew,
I enter the realm of 'What to do?'
Cooking disasters, a comedy show,
In my safe space, I steal the show.

Boundaries of Serenity

Cushions piled high, the throne of me,
In this kingdom, I hold the key.
Outside may shine with hustle and grind,
But here, relaxation I will find.

The door is locked, it's me-time bliss,
A world away from the daily hiss.
In pajamas, I'm a queen by right,
With popcorn in hand, oh what a sight!

The Embraces We Create

In a snug corner, I find my snack,
While my cat plans a stealthy attack.
The couch is my throne, my cereal's crown,
Oh, the joys of not wearing a frown!

Binge-watching shows, laughter fills the air,
Glad my replays don't require a pair.
With popcorn explosions and soda spills,
Who needs the world when you've got these thrills?

Solitude's Gentle Repose

In solitude's arms, I take a nap,
While dreams weave stories in a cozy trap.
My blanket's a fort, my pillow a wall,
Defending my snooze from the world's loud call.

Socks mismatched, I dance 'round the room,
In this little bubble, there's never gloom.
The cat gives me looks, as if I'm insane,
But who needs the norm? I'll go dance in the rain!

A Safe Retreat

Behind these doors, I choose to hide,
With snacks piled high, and slippers wide.
The world can wait, I'll take my time,
In this fortress of snacks, everything's sublime.

Emails pile up, but I won't check,
I'm tight with my couch like an old school deck.
With a mug of cocoa, I'll never feel blue,
Who needs the outside? I've got comfy shoes!

Challenges Beyond the Threshold

The door's an abyss, a leap of faith,
Outside lies chaos, my personal wraith.
Yet here in my fortress, I'm big and bold,
Where my snack cabinet's a treasure of gold.

They say life's a journey, but I'm just fine,
With reruns and snacks, I'll just recline.
Why venture forth, when I can embrace,
The wonders of lounging in my own space?

Hearthstone Dreams

In a chair so soft, I hear a snore,
My cat's on my lap, what a cozy chore.
The TV's on mute, the chips all gone,
Yet somehow, the party's just begun!

With socks on my feet, I dance in my head,
Fueled by the snacks, I should really have fled.
In dreams, I'm a hero, on quests all night,
But first, I'll just finish this slice of delight!

Sheltered in Silence

A blanket fort made of pillows and sheets,
Whispers of laughter, my heart skips a beat.
Outside, there's chaos, but here I must stay,
With snacks piled up high, I can't run away!

Old cartoons play on the screen in my mind,
The world out there, oh so unrefined.
Here, I'm a giant, a king on a throne,
In my quiet kingdom, I'm never alone!

The Cloister of Content

A cup of hot cocoa, my royal decree,
My kingdom is cozy, just my cat and me.
In mismatched slippers, I roam my domain,
Not a care in the world, just joy in the rain!

With board games piled high, I rule this retreat,
A king in my castle where everything's sweet.
I may be a hermit, but don't feel left out,
When laughter comes knocking, I'll let it shout!

Boundaries of Belonging

With pizza delivery, I seal my fate,
Never too early to celebrate!
In pajamas all day, I reign supreme,
Finding joy in the silliest of dreams.

A bubble of giggles, a realm all my own,
Here I can laugh, absolutely alone.
With friends on the phone, I'm never apart,
Together we giggle, it warms up my heart!

Soothing Retirements

In slippers soft, they slide and glide,
With snacks galore, they turn the tide.
The yoga mats gather dust anew,
While couch potatoes dream of stew.

Remote controls are their best friends,
As weekend chaos surely ends.
The garden's neat, but full of weeds,
A perfect place for lazy deeds.

Naps are sacred, don't you dare!
The recliners creak, but they don't care.
With mugs of tea that never cool,
They've found their joy in comfy rule.

So raise a toast to lazy days,
With little fuss and lots of rays.
Their soothing life is what we crave,
In every nap, a tiny wave.

The Gentle Boundaries of Love

In cozy nooks, they share a glance,
With playful pokes, they take a chance.
A quilt of quirks wraps 'round their hearts,
While laughter plays its silly parts.

She steals the last piece of the pie,
And blames the cat with a cheeky sigh.
A dance-off in the kitchen space,
Where burnt bread sings, a charming grace.

They bicker sweetly, nothing mean,
As crumbs of joy become their scene.
With laughter loud and mischief bright,
Their gentle walls bring pure delight.

So here's to love, with all its quirks,
In life's ballet, the fun just lurks.
Each silly message on the fridge,
Shows that they've crossed the best of bridges.

Shadows of Sweet Assurance

In every corner, echoes hum,
Of jests exchanged, and playful fun.
The cookie jar is always bare,
With snack attacks that can't compare.

A paper airplane flies up high,
As giggles dance into the sky.
The living room, a battle zone,
Where laughter reigns, and joy has grown.

A shadow wanders, always near,
With whispered jokes to share a cheer.
As movie nights unfold with glee,
Their silly hearts can't help but be.

So let them bask in silly glee,
With shadows thick and spirits free.
In every chuckle, a secret shared,
Their cozy life, brilliantly paired.

Hearths of Hope

With mugs in hand, they tell tall tales,
Of adventures grand and floppy sails.
Each crackling fire, a heart's embrace,
As stories spin in every space.

The cat yawns wide, he's heard it all,
While tiny feet begin to crawl.
With chocolate crumbs on every face,
They share their dreams in playful grace.

The bubble baths are filled with laughs,
As rubber ducks play ancient drafts.
Tickles, giggles, the sounds of joy,
In each warm day, a brand new ploy.

So here's to cheer in every nook,
With hopeful hearts on every hook.
In hearths of hope, they find their way,
Their silly lives, a bright bouquet.

Encircled by Calm

A fortress of pillows, a blanket's embrace,
Where snacks are the currency, life's simple grace.
In pajamas we lounge, on couches we lay,
Turning chores into jokes, prolonging the day.

Remote in one hand, the other a treat,
Life's challenges fade, oh, isn't this neat?
With laughter and giggles, we create our own space,
In a kingdom of comfort, we find our own place.

Warmth in Enclosure

In a nook made for laughter, we cackle with cheer,
Fuzzy socks on our feet, while the world disappears.
Like squirrels in a den, hoarding popcorn galore,
We munch and we giggle, who could ask for more?

The radio croons softly, with hits from the past,
Our worries are jokes, they never can last.
With every silly story that sparks in the air,
We find joy in this bubble, no troubles to share.

The Breach of Safety

Oh, the world outside calls, with its hustle and strife,
But who needs the chaos when we've perfected this life?
With a slip and a slide, oh dear, what a fall!
Tripping over the dog, we all laugh till we sprawl.

When chores come a-knocking, we hide and we jest,
Pretending we're busy, oh, we're truly the best!
With snacks piled high, we perform our grand show,
The remote's our scepter, in comfort we glow.

The Shield of Stillness

Behind cozy barriers, we let laughter fly,
Wi-Fi our magic, as hours drift by.
In the realm of the couch, we weave our own tale,
With tales of remarkable feats, oh boy, we'll regale!

Every knock on the door feels like a prank,
"Who wants to join us?" we holler, all blank.
In our bubble of giggles, we reign as the kings,
Wrapped in our lives, oh, the joy that it brings!

Embraces of the Known

In cozy nooks where secrets lie,
The pizza's cold, the cat's high and dry.
We sing off-key with utmost glee,
And celebrate normal—just you and me.

Each chair's a throne, our drinks are bold,
While we tell tales that never get old.
In this sweet bubble, we jest and tease,
And contemplate all our favorite cheese.

The floor is sticky, the lights are dim,
Our fashion choices are slightly grim.
But here's the catch: we really don't care,
It's all about laughter we gladly share.

Like clowns in a tent, brightly adorned,
With every mishap, we laugh till we're worn.
So here's to comfort, quirky and bright,
In a world of oddities, all feels just right.

Still Waters of Conformity

In matching socks and khaki shorts,
We blend like peas in silly reports.
We sit in rows, our heads all nod,
To the same old tune, it's a bit of a façade.

The coffee brews with every hour,
While we engage in daily power.
Deadpan jokes about life's routine,
Like robots stuck in a feedback machine.

We all pretend to follow the rules,
Yet dance in circles like silly fools.
In this calm sea where laughter flows,
The chaos beneath is where the fun grows.

Unruly giggles in a stoic guise,
A winking world behind buttoned-up ties.
Let's raise our mugs to monotony's thrill,
For in these waters, we find our own chill.

Harbors of Tranquility

Boat drinks in hands, we settle in,
Like seasoned sailors, our chairs we pin.
The gossip flows like a gentle tide,
With seashell confessions and hearts open wide.

Amidst the calm, we roast our mates,
From wacky hats to crooked plates.
With a wink here and a nudge there,
Life is a circus we gladly share.

We joke about storms that never come,
While secretly hoping for a little fun.
Each wave of laughter brings us peace,
In this funny harbor, worries decrease.

Like dolphins leaping through playful waves,
We find joy in silliness that saves.
Let's anchor down and sip our tea,
In this calm bay, just you and me.

Veils of Acceptance

In comfy chairs, we drape our pain,
With blanket forts that hold our disdain.
We wear our quirks like a badge of pride,
And laugh at our flaws, we won't ever hide.

Like puzzle pieces that fit just so,
In the grand charade where laughter will flow.
Our mismatched socks walk hand in hand,
In this cozy kingdom, we boldly stand.

We dance in pajamas, a sight unseen,
With cups of coffee and a movie machine.
And who needs rules when we've got charm?
With funny stories that keep us warm.

Acceptance drapes like a colorful quilt,
No judgments here, only laughter built.
So let's revel in our oddball spree,
And embrace the weird—just you and me.

Horizons of Home

In a fortress made of socks,
And a moat of empty mugs,
I find treasures that shock,
In this castle of snuggly hugs.

The windows, they're just screens,
With memes pouring in from afar,
I wave at my plant, it leans,
My only knight, my home-grown star.

The fridge is a dragon, fierce,
Guarding snacks with fiery breath,
I raid it with stealth, then pierce,
The ice cream - my dessert's death.

In this kingdom of cozy fluff,
My throne is just a chair, quite worn,
Yet the king still feels quite tough,
In a court where laughter is born.

Ramps of Respite

I glide down the couch like a slide,
A bump here, a wiggle there,
The remote's my trusty guide,
On this journey of comfy flair.

Pajamas, my royal dress,
With pockets aplenty for snacks,
I run this realm with finesse,
No need for armor, just relax.

The rug has become my sea,
Where I sail on pillows afloat,
In a ship made of tea,
I navigate dreams, keeping note.

Here every corner's a nook,
Where kittens conspire with yarn,
I find my best storybook,
In a world where no one feels worn.

Ensnared in Embrace

Wrapped in a blanket burrito,
With chips as my trusty shield,
I munch as I watch the video,
Of a cat that can dance and wield.

Each cushion a hug from the past,
They whisper tales of my glee,
In this snuggly fortress, I blast,
Fun shows 'til the day's decree.

When I tumble off the couch,
I pretend it's a daring leap,
From this wasabi-green pouch,
My laughs echo while cats snooze deep.

Yet, here in my haven profound,
I'm a noble couch potato king,
Where laughter and joy abound,
And to life's dance, I still cling.

The Gentle Barrier

A fortress of laundry piles high,
Where shirts play the role of walls,
I peek out to watch the sky,
While my snack drawer softly calls.

With pillows as my trusty steed,
I venture forth, just a few feet,
In this kingdom, I plant my seed,
Chocolate rivers flow to my seat.

The doorbell rings, and I flee,
Under sheets with a pillow mask,
In a quest as grand as can be,
To avoid just the simplest task.

Yet here in my cocoon of bliss,
Where giggles dance on every wall,
Each moment's a comfy kiss,
In my gentle fortress, I'm enthralled.

Hiding in Soft Corners

In a chair that hugs my shape,
I vanish like a wary ape.
Pillows piled up to the sky,
A fortress where no frown can lie.

Socks become my loyal guards,
As I nap behind the shards.
Waves of laughter, snacks galore,
Who needs much, when sleep's in store?

My blanket's like a magic spell,
With cozy vibes, I laugh, oh swell!
To friends I wave with muffled glee,
"Join me here, it's unbothered spree!"

In corners soft, we shall reside,
Where worries fade, and joy's our guide.
The world outside can stand and wait,
In my plush realm, I'm truly great!

The Veil of Familiarity

Tea mugs clink like secret spies,
In corners familiar, laughter flies.
Each creak of floor, a friend's embrace,
In cozy nooks, we find our place.

Slippers shuffle, a dance so grand,
In a rhythm that we all understand.
Who needs the wild? We have our shows,
Popcorn fights, as the evening glows.

The remote control, our scepter of power,
Decisions ruled from comfy tower.
Couch cushions stacked like balmy hills,
In this realm, absurdity fulfills.

Familiar walls, they wrap us tight,
In every corner, pure delight.
With witty chats that never tire,
Our laughter's the spark, our bliss is the fire!

Brick by Brick, We Build

Brick by brick, we lay our day,
In a fortress made of games and play.
Each laugh is mortar, every sigh a stone,
In this goofy place, we're never alone.

We stack our cushions, high and proud,
Creating a citadel, laughter loud.
Cardboard castles, they won't fall,
When silly jokes echo through these halls.

Each snack a treasure, we hoard with glee,
Donuts and cookies—a sweet decree.
With mugs of cocoa, we toast to this,
A life of comfort, oh, what a bliss!

From piles of laundry to nature's hiss,
In our cozy nook, there's endless bliss.
Step outside? Well, that's too bold,
In this haven, our hearts unfold!

Enclaves of Ease

In corners tucked, we plot and scheme,
With cups of joy, we weave our dream.
A world outside feels far away,
In our enclaves of ease, we choose to stay.

Socks with holes form our secret code,
As we lounge on couches, life's abode.
The fridge, a treasure chest indeed,
Where snacks are plenty, fulfilling every need.

Friendship flows like a fizzy drink,
In quirky moments, we laugh and wink.
Pajamas on, it's our fashion show,
In goofy poses, we all steal the show.

With laughter tight, we softly pray,
For this blissful state, forever to stay.
So raise a glass, let joy release,
In our zones of fun, we find our peace!

Nests of Caring Spirits

In corners snug, we find our cheer,
Where laughter dances, bright and clear.
Old socks and chairs with tales to tell,
Turn frowns to giggles, all is well.

Cushions piled like mountain peaks,
Tickled pink, and laughter squeaks.
Banana peel on floor's parade,
A slippery slip, a comical cascade!

The tea pot whistles, a merry tune,
As I prance around like a dancing loon.
Snack crumbs gather, a furry feast,
Where all are welcome, even the beast.

So join the fun, relinquish stress,
In this cozy nest, we're all a mess.
With friends like these, joy never parts,
In nests of caring, we stash our hearts.

A Shield of Whispers

Beneath the roof, secrets take flight,
Chit-chats echo through the night.
With pillows plush, we giggle and snicker,
As the fridge hums tunes, I sneak a snicker.

A blanket fort, a fortress wide,
Where jokes like popcorn bounce inside.
Guarded by whispers, we plot our schemes,
And share the wildest of our dreams.

Repurposed boxes become our throne,
As we laugh at the pizza we've overgrown.
In this laughter, we fear no spies,
With every chuckle, our worries defies.

So give a hoot, let loose the glee,
In whispered realms, we're fancy and free.
A shield of laughter, a joyous sound,
Where comfort's armor so easily found.

The Hearth and Heart

Gather round the crackling fire,
Where stories spark and never tire.
The marshmallows fluff, a sugary treat,
As we roast them golden, our giggles sweet.

Chairs awash in colors bright,
We gather close, a silly sight.
With board games sprawled and snacks galore,
An epic battle, who keeps the score?

With each small joke, the ember glows,
Sharing woes, and striking poses.
The clock ticks on, yet we won't part,
For joy resides at the hearth of the heart.

In this cozy space, we're never alone,
With voices swirling, love's our own.
Laughter lingers as shadows dart,
Nestled within this gleeful art.

Quietude's Keep

In quiet corners, we share our dreams,
Where silliness flows in bubbling streams.
Woolly socks and floppy hats,
Become the finest of all our chats.

With drowsy eyes, we sip our brew,
Dreaming up worlds both silly and new.
The cat's on guard; he hears our plans,
As we plot adventures with wild hand spans.

Crack the code of noodle arms,
And dance in place, oh what a charm!
Silent disco, with socks adorned,
In quietude's keep, we are reborn.

So cherish these moments, blissful and neat,
In our little enclave, life's bittersweet.
With laughter as armor, together we leap,
In the magic of silence, we find our keep.

Resting Beneath Familiar Canopies

Beneath the trees, the squirrels play,
Their acorn stash grows day by day.
A hammock swings, I sip my drink,
The world outside, I barely think.

The birds are gossiping above,
While I plot ways to eat, and shove.
Sunbeams slip through leafy lanes,
As laughter dances, joy remains.

With snacks galore, I take my seat,
In nature's lap, life feels complete.
A nap might follow in this bliss,
Oh, how I savor moments like this!

Familiar sights, a cozy scene,
The tired cat sprawls, she's quite the queen.
In this retreat, I find my cheer,
If only chores would disappear!

The Silent Sanctuary

In cozy caves where whispers dwell,
I hide from life, oh what a spell!
The laundry's piled, the dishes too,
Yet here I sit, just me and stew.

A chair that squeaks, a smile it brings,
As I debate on funny things.
The tv hums a silly show,
Fuzzy slippers steal the glow.

Out there, the bustle, here I rest,
With chocolate treats, I feel the best.
The world can wait, let it take pause,
For this sweet couch has earned applause!

In my domain, I reign supreme,
With midnight snacks, I boldly dream.
Tomorrow's chaos, it can wait,
For right now, it's just me and fate!

Enclosed by Kindness

A blanket fort made of love and care,
With snacks and jokes, who wouldn't dare?
The kids all giggle, they're having fun,
While I sip tea under the sun.

The walls may wobble, the roof might droop,
But here we form our cozy troop.
A wild adventure in every glance,
We thrive in chaos, we laugh and dance.

With toys and dreams all piled high,
In this fortress we watch time fly.
Battling boredom or mundane strife,
Wrapped in warmth, we're full of life.

While nature calls from far away,
I'll take my time, let me just stay.
For kindness lingers, ever strong,
In this small world, we all belong!

Elysium of the Everyday

With every cup of morning brew,
The laughter spills, it feels so new.
In this routine, hilarity blooms,
As socks go missing, and dust resumes.

A cat that trips over her own tail,
A shoe that squeaks, a jolly tale.
The chaos wraps me like a song,
In ordinary things, we all belong.

I trip on laundry, what a sight,
The vacuum roars, it gives a fright.
Yet peace pours in with every grin,
In this sweet circus, we laugh and spin.

So here we dance, among the mess,
Finding magic in each small stress.
To live, to love, to find the cheer,
In daily blunders, we persevere!

Shelters of the Heart

In a quilt of snacks I hide,
Wrapped in chips, chips like pride.
Laughter echoes, bites of glee,
Here I sit, just me and me.

Cousin Bob slipped on a shoe,
Said it felt like winter's dew.
I chuckled while he took a spill,
In our cozy, comfy thrill.

With pillows stacked as high as clouds,
We giggle, joke, and wear our shrouds.
A fortress made of fluff and cheer,
Where silly thoughts run far and near.

Peeking out from every nook,
As the world outside just shook.
In my safe haven, all is bright,
Where crazy antics take their flight.

The Sanctuary Within

In a chair that creaks and sways,
I ponder life in funny ways.
Cereal for dinner, what a treat,
In this nook, I can't be beat!

My cat, the judge, sits with a glare,
While I dance like I have no care.
He thinks I'm bonkers, oh so bad,
But in my world, I'm just a lad.

In socks that don't quite match the hue,
I prance about, yes, that's my cue.
The walls are laughing, can you hear?
Inside this bubble, there's no fear.

As I gather all my dreams and quirks,
Amongst the clutter, joy lurks.
Waving goodbye to daily strife,
In my zone, I live my life.

Comfort's Gentle Veil

With slippers on that squeak and slide,
    I giggle at my silly pride.
While cookies crumble all around,
    In sugar-coated joy, I'm found.

A bean bag throne, my royal seat,
I rule this realm of snacks and treats.
The TV blares, a sitcom's scene,
My laughter blends, a joyful screen.

When cousin Jane starts doing tricks,
    We roll around, our laughter kicks.
With every joke and silly line,
    We add some sparkle to our dine.

Beneath this gentle, cozy quilt,
    A world of laughter is built.
While outside storms might pelt and pound,
    Inside my fun zone, joy is found.

Edges of Familiarity

In pajamas worn with pride I stroll,
Amidst the snacks, I feel so whole.
Where routines mingle, laugh, and dance,
In my silly world, I take a chance.

A rubber chicken at my side,
No worries here, oh how I ride!
Every knock-knock joke is gold,
Our humor never gets too old.

I trade my shoes for funky socks,
While doodling on cardboard boxes.
A fortress built of laughter loud,
Where I'm the queen and wear my crown.

From binge-watching shows to silly pranks,
We share the laughs, we raise our ranks.
In this space where friendship stays,
We savor life's most joyful ways.

Boundaries Conceal

Within my room, I dance with glee,
In corner shadows, just me and me.
The cat on guard, a silent knight,
Judging my moves with a sideways fright.

I built a wall of pillows and fluff,
Which cushions my dreams, though times get tough.
When friends drop by, they roll their eyes,
"Is this the party?" they feign surprise.

Loud laughter echoes, I give them a peek,
Through my fortress tall, they hear me squeak.
A throne of socks, so proud I reign,
My kingdom of comfort, both joyful and plain.

But if I trip on my own cozy spree,
The laughter's on me, I can hardly see.
Yet in this soft world, I feel so grand,
Unruly ruler of my fluffy land.

Nurture Reveal

Nestled in cushions, my safe little nook,
Where snacks and giggles are all it took.
I cradle my secrets wrapped in a pie,
As dreams of grand feasts make the time fly.

With my blanket fort, I'm queen of the night,
Each corner a treasure, a joyful sight.
When the popcorn's spilled, it's a sight so sweet,
A buttery scene that can't be beat!

I serenade walls with a silly little tune,
While the cat joins in, thinking he's a raccoon.
The dance of the dust bunnies starts anew,
While I giggle at shadows that twist into two.

So waltz in my realm, fueled by whimsy's delight,
Where clumsy missteps become pure insight.
With laughter as fuel and nutty dreams spun,
In this hidden retreat, life's just begun!

Serenity's Silent Cradle

In a realm where socks become a mound,
I weave my dreams without a bound.
Snuggled tight in a sea of threads,
With visions of unicorns dancing in my head.

The kettle whispers tales of tea,
While I contemplate all things carefree.
My mind drifts off to whimsical heights,
As the pancake stack teeters in flights!

The clock ticks loud in its playful tease,
I toast bread to victory, or so it seems.
While crumbs play hopscotch all over the floor,
This joyful chaos leaves me wanting more.

The serenity found in my jumbled design,
Turns simple moments into something divine.
With laughter so sweet, I serenade the day,
In my cozy domain, it's too fun to stray!

Untouched Corners of the Heart

In the attic of thought, dust bunnies roam,
They laugh at the places I call my home.
Each untouched corner, a story untold,
A treasure chest waiting, with memories old.

The cookie jar sits, a guardian so proud,
Whispering softly, "Shall we share with the crowd?"
But I chuckle and cringe at the looming delight,
As I vow to savor them, just out of sight.

Every quirkiness hid, like socks gone astray,
Bringing giggles with every silly play.
The heart grows bright, in this playful refrain,
For untouched moments make joy entertain.

So come tread gently on this whimsied space,
With laughter that dances, setting the pace.
In corners neglected, let chuckles ignite,
A heart full of wonder, gleaming and bright.

Echoes from the Enclosure

In the cocoon where hilarity brews,
Echoes of laughter, a rhythmic muse.
As I imitate squirrels, twirling with glee,
The walls hold my giggles, just wait and see!

With snacks on the table, oh what a sight,
Chips cling to fingers, oh dear, what a plight!
I dive into dips, lose all sense of grace,
Embarking on crumbles, this messy embrace.

Each echo a memory, each laugh a sound,
The walls hoarding jokes, a bond tightly wound.
As we sip on juice boxes, it's kid time for sure,
The whispers of comfort create an allure.

So here in my bubble, don't be in a rush,
For each moment's a giggle, a giggly hush.
Within this snug hub, where hearts dance unchained,
Echoes of joy in my fortress remained.

Edges of Surrender

In a bubble, snug and round,
I lost my keys, they can't be found.
Beneath my snack stash, I recline,
Why bother moving? This is divine!

My couch is a sea of crumbs and chips,
A fortress built with epic quips.
Why face the world when Netflix calls?
I've found my kingdom, within these walls.

Pajamas are my royal attire,
With snacks galore, I've built my fire.
The fridge is close, my throne is set,
This lazy dream, I won't regret!

So let them judge, those busy bees,
I'll wave from here, with all my ease.
To each their quest, but here I'll stay,
In this cozy nook, I found my way.

The Cocoon of Clarity

Wrapped in blankets, snug and warm,
I ponder life, its wild charm.
The world outside feels far away,
In this cozy space, I'm free to play.

The mysteries of socks unfold,
Where did one go? I can't be told.
Are they hiding, just for kicks?
In this soft trap, I'm feeling slick!

My tea is steeping, dreams take flight,
As I plot my dinner with delight.
Clarity comes in sips and bites,
In my snug realm, I see the lights.

So wrap me up, in this cocoon,
Where the distant world feels like a tune.
I'll dance with thoughts, with laughter loud,
In this silly space, I feel so proud.

Refuge of Reassurance

In a blanket fort of faded sheets,
I find my joy, life's little treats.
Outside the window, chaos reigns,
But in my nest, I'll ignore the trains.

With every chip and soda pop,
I think I might just never stop.
The remote's my wand, magic in hand,
As sitcom laughter makes my stand.

Pillows piled, a mountain true,
My laughter echoing, how about you?
In this land of snacks and mirth,
I reign supreme, my simple turf.

So let the storm clouds roll and moan,
In my fortress here, I'm never alone.
With friends on screen, I take my seat,
In this warm cave, I'm oh so sweet.

Cultivating Comfort

With a teacup perched on my lap,
I study the art of a cozy nap.
The world demands, but I just chuckle,
My blanket's tight, I feel the snuggle.

A plant in the corner, slowly droops,
Just like me, we're lazy troops.
Watering can? A distant dream,
In this comfort zone, life's supreme.

Bad hair days? I'm blissfully free,
Who needs mirrors, when I can just be?
In this lazy haze, I find my song,
With every giggle, I know I belong.

So here I'll stay, my happy space,
Laughing at life, with style and grace.
I'll cultivate joy, like a garden bright,
In this perfect nook, my heart takes flight.

The Trust of Known Paths

In slippers worn and coffee brewed,
I dance through shadows, not subdued.
The cat knows better, twitches a paw,
While I trip over yesterday's straw.

The fridge hums tunes of ancient delights,
A dance with leftovers—what a sight!
I swear the carrots have started to glow,
As I ponder which sauce to throw.

The couch is a throne, my royal seat,
Where crumbs and laughs compete to greet.
With cushions that swallow, I'm lost in the fluff,
Who needs adventure when comfort's enough?

In corners where laughter and socks collide,
Life's little chaos becomes my guide.
With giggles and sighs, I rest my case,
On this merry journey, I find my space.

Comfort's Cloaked Corners

In cozy nooks where dust bunnies play,
I find all my treasures from yesterday.
A half-eaten cookie, an old magazine,
Together they weave a whimsical scene.

The laundry pile laughs, a towering feat,
As socks stage a coup to claim my seat.
With every tumble, a sock's secret plots,
While I debate if they're lost or just knots.

The tea kettle whistles a curious tune,
Inviting me over at quarter to noon.
I sip with a smile, mustache of foam,
This is my kingdom, this striped cotton dome.

Oh, laughter echoes and giggles reside,
Within these four walls, my comforts abide.
No need for the world when I have my chair,
Comfy and giggling, I'm free as air.

Home's Embrace

As curtains flutter like flags in a breeze,
Every creak and groan is a friend who agrees.
The plants are gossiping, their leaves in a sway,
While I ponder if there's life outside today.

The dog gives a sigh, stretches on the rug,
His dreams involve bones, not a daily slug.
With every sigh, my worries unwind,
At home's warm embrace, peace is refined.

The carpet's a stage, where dust bunnies dance,
As I spin around in a careless prance.
With quirky routines, I'm a star on my own,
In this humble abode, I've easily grown.

Laughter's my language as I declutter each room,
From boxes of memories to the old vacuum.
With a wink and a nod, I savor each day,
In this laugh-filled space, I find my way.

Whispered Comforts

In secretive whispers, the walls tend to speak,
Of midnight snacks and adventures unique.
The fridge opens wide, an impatient fellow,
Can't resist the allure of that chocolate marshmallow.

The old chair creaks tales of days long gone,
Of marathons watched till the very last dawn.
Each cushion a memory, soft as a dream,
Where comfort's a painter, crafting my theme.

The world outside may be fast and loud,
But here in my cocoon, I'm comfort-proud.
Pajamas my armor, I roam like a knight,
In quest of the perfect couch for the night.

So raise your tea cups to layers of fun,
Where giggles and cushions unite as one.
In corners we gather, our joys intertwine,
Whispering secrets like a glass of fine wine.

The Refuge of Enduring Echoes

In my cozy nook where echoes creep,
The chocolate stash is mine to keep.
Socks on the floor in a fashion parade,
Who needs a runway when comfort's made?

The laundry talks, oh what a friend,
It knows my secrets, until the end.
Spilled coffee dances on the chair,
Each stain a memory, beyond compare.

My plant thinks I'm a stand-up comic,
Its leaves are laughing, somewhat ironic.
Giddy shadows play in the corner light,
Making the mundane, such a delight.

So here's to laughter, soft and light,
In my little haven, everything's right.
The comfort of chaos is quite the charm,
Wrapped in my blankets, I'm safe from harm.

Tender Spaces

In the couch's embrace, the cushions conspire,
To hold all my snacks, and igniting my fire.
TV reruns call, their voices a tease,
I laugh at their jokes, with adorable ease.

My fondest of pillows, they know all my woes,
In the space between dreams, the snoring just flows.
Each midnight snack is a joyous delight,
With crumbs in my lap, a delicious sight.

The blanket's a fortress, so snug and so warm,
Within this cocoon, I weather the storm.
Slippers like clouds on my feet, oh so divine,
Life's little treasures, in moments so fine.

So here's to my realm where smiles never cease,
With tenderness woven into life's fleece.
Laughter is louder than washing machine hum,
In these tender spaces, joy always comes.

Sheltered Whispers

Between the four walls where shadows play,
Whispers of laughter, they never decay.
The fridge hums a tune, a soft serenade,
While leftovers whisper, 'We won't be delayed.'

In the corner, dust bunnies hold their court,
While I plot their escape, my own little sport.
I giggle with glee at their fluffy ballet,
Performing their antics, what a fine display!

Cafe of comfort, where tea cups rejoice,
Each sip a small giggle, a cheerful voice.
I've mastered the art of a blanket-induced nap,
With the pillows aligned, I'm caught in the tap.

So in this sweet cocoon, chaos seems far,
With whispers of joy, I'm the shining star.
Finding humor in moments, I'm clever and spry,
In sheltered embraces where laughter can fly.

The Familiarity of Safety

In my favorite chair, where days slip by,
A classic sitcom makes me sigh.
Popcorn in hand, I relish each jest,
In this bubble of joy, I find my rest.

Fuzzy socks roaming on tiles all day,
Little mischief-makers in their own way.
Under the blanket, they do a fine jig,
Trying to tickle my toes, oh so big!

The clock on the wall ticks its routine,
Each second a chuckle, life's sweetest scene.
I toast to the couch, with a fizzy delight,
For home is my humor, wrapped in soft light.

So here's to the moments that tickle the heart,
In the familiarity, I play my part.
With laughter as fuel and joy by my side,
In this safe little haven, I take great pride.

A Fortress of Familiarity

In my chair, I munch away,
The dog steals snacks without delay.
TV blares, I clash with sleep,
But cozy's grand, it's all on repeat.

Pjs drape like a soft cocoon,
Socks unmatched, like a cartoon.
Coffee spills, I laugh and sigh,
Life's a mess, but I can't deny.

Friends pop in, snacks on hand,
We plot the world from our sofa land.
Giggles echo through the room,
Who cares if dishes start to bloom?

Mismatched decor, a plastic plant,
I call it art; my friends just chant.
A fortress built on laughter's glee,
I wouldn't trade this life for free!

Nestled in Tranquility

Blankets tangled, I find my zone,
Cats are sprawled, we rule our throne.
With chips and dip, it's all so bright,
Tranquil chaos, pure delight.

The neighbors yell, I hear the cheer,
I wave and laugh, my couch holds dear.
A fortress of cushions, snacks galore,
I'll never leave through that front door.

Sunlight drapes like a golden veil,
We sing off-key, we never pale.
Some call it nuts, others call it home,
In our bubble, we safely roam.

Lazy days, we nap and feed,
In this la-la-land, we all succeed.
Who needs a castle, wide and grand?
This sofa's the best in all the land!

The Embrace of the Known

I keep my cereal on a chair,
Spill it once, I just don't care.
Movies rerun, plots align,
Spoiler alert? Not this time!

Pajamas reign, fashion's a joke,
In slippers soft, I'm fully woke.
Pizza boxes tell a tale,
Of feasts and fun, we shall not fail.

The fridge hums a familiar tune,
I grab leftovers instead of a spoon.
Here in this chaos, blissfully grown,
With laughter and snacks, I'm never alone.

Every corner has a memory stored,
Of wine nights and laughs, together adored.
Life's an oddball, jokes on repeat,
But in this embrace, I feel complete!

Surroundings of Solace

My sofa's a ship, the remote's my oar,
In this sea of snacks, I explore.
The dog sighs loud, gives me the eye,
Is it time for treats? Oh my, oh my!

Neighbors bicker about the lawn,
While I dive deep into the dawn.
Here comes a squirrel, cheeky and bold,
My heart's a pirate, my ship's pure gold.

Tea spills, it stains the rug,
I shrug it off, just another hug.
Surrounded by laughter, in comfy attire,
This chaotic solace, my heart's desire.

We dance in pajamas, lyrics all wrong,
In this wacky space, we truly belong.
With joy as our armor, we laugh through the night,
In these surroundings, everything feels right!

In the Arms of Solace

In a chair that hugs my shape,
Propped with pillows, it's my escape.
Sipping tea in my robe so wide,
I reign as queen, with snacks as my guide.

The dog rolls by, with graceful flair,
He thinks he owns this cozy square.
A cat joins in, with a smug little grin,
Together we plot how to never begin.

The socks, mismatched, on my feet,
A fashion statement, bittersweet.
Laughter echoes, a ticklish cheer,
As I ponder, "What's for lunch, my dear?"

So here's to solace, wrapped in delight,
Where every meal feels just right.
I laugh with walls that don't judge my ways,
In my fortress of joy, I dream the days.

Zones of Emotive Ease

There's a nook, a favorite chair,
With its cushions worn, I hold no care.
Books piled high, that hasn't been read,
Yet here I sit, with thoughts in my head.

An old lamp flickers with a dramatic flare,
Casting shadows that dance in the air.
The fridge hums softly, a friendly tune,
While outside neighbors argue at noon.

Pajamas on, all day long,
In this bliss, I sing my song.
Socks on my hands for warmth and grace,
As I giggle at life's silly race.

Here's to moments of pure delight,
With each giggle echoing bright.
Behind these doors, I find my ease,
Life's quirks wrapped up, like a cozy breeze.

Calmness Beyond the Threshold

In fluffy slippers, I stroll about,
In a land where worries swim and pout.
The plants look on with leafy cheer,
As I share my troubles with iced root beer.

The clock ticks slow, almost to tease,
While I stuff my face with gooey cheese.
The chair, a throne, holds my tired bones,
As cartoons blare in cheerful tones.

Quirky mugs line my precious shelf,
Each one a memory, of my past self.
They witness my mischief, my whimsy and spark,
In a kingdom so comfy, my own little ark.

With laughter ringing, my heart is light,
In these walls, nothing feels contrite.
Just a giggle, a snack, a playful dive,
In this space, is where I thrive.

A Tapestry of Safety

My couch is a cloud, plush and deep,
Where every nap turns into sleep.
A blanket fortress, pulled up to my chin,
Where dreams take flight, adventures begin.

Remote control in my reigning grasp,
With channels galore, I hide and gasp.
Popcorn spills, my guilty delight,
As I chuckle at silliness, day turns to night.

The wall art winks, full of jest,
Each print tells tales of the very best.
Dust bunnies twirl, with a mischievous grin,
As I shuffle by, they let the fun spin.

So here I dwell, in humor dressed,
In this tapestry, I count my blessed.
With laughter ringing and spilt cheers,
I bask in the joy of my simple years.

Hearth of Tender Memories

In my cozy nook, I find my chair,
With old cat socks, and frizzy hair.
Each snack I nibble, crumbs galore,
Echo laughter from days before.

The walls may wobble with secrets untold,
Of dreams that shimmer, and tales bold.
I dance like a duck, in my fuzzy socks,
Time slips away, like forgotten clocks.

My fridge hums tunes from long ago,
A symphony of leftovers, in a row.
With a slice of cake, and a cup of tea,
I toast to bliss, oh let it be!

So here I dwell, with quirks of pride,
A haven for the odd, not meant to hide.
In weirdness, I bubble, like soda pop,
In my hearth of wonders, I'll never stop.

Horizons Within Shadows

In corners cuddled, shadows sway,
With dust bunnies plotting a grand getaway.
A rock band of mice, they strum and hum,
While underneath my couch I'm feeling numb.

Oh, the ceiling paints a tale so surreal,
Of upside-down worlds, and a pizza meal.
I spy the clock, it's mocking my stare,
Time's a trickster, floating in mid-air.

A blanket fort pinned with dreams old,
I sip on juice, feeling feisty and bold.
Each corner hides whispers of glee,
In this land of misfits, just me and me.

So let the shadows dance, let them prance,
With silly antics, they take their chance.
In this cozy chaos, I choose to stay,
A monarch of laughter in my disarray.

Cloistered by Familiarity

In my little realm, the socks don't match,
Each pile of laundry hides a hilarious catch.
The coffee pot gurgles an old-time tune,
While I trip on my shoes, in the afternoon.

The fridge is a canvas, art made of cheese,
With experiments in yogurt that surely tease.
Life's a circus in my cluttered space,
With bubbling giggles that always embrace.

I chat with my plants, they nod with glee,
While a wayward fly thinks it's truly free.
A parade of quirks fills my cozy bear den,
Where mischief and giggles matter—again and again!

So here's to the laughter, it's never so wrong,
In the quilt of my life, it stitches a song.
With cushions of dreams, I lay down my head,
In this joyful chaos, I'm perfectly wed.

Inner Respite

At the heart of my castle, the TV glows bright,
Worn pillows fly as I'm ready for flight.
The couch is a ship, sailing dream-like seas,
With snacks as my cargo, and laughter as breeze.

Each flicker of news brings a smile and a sigh,
As I channel-surf through a cloud in the sky.
The remote—my magic wand, raucous and wild,
In my cozy kingdom, I'm forever a child.

Friends in the frames, with stories that weave,
Bound by mischief that no one can leave.
A dance party erupts with meals in my lap,
As my living room turns to a dazzling map.

So here I giggle, in my pajama delight,
With voices from sitcoms keeping me bright.
In this hug of oddity, perfectly clear,
My heart swells with joy; oh, how I need here!

Corners of Quietude

In the nook where pillows lay,
I sip my drink, it's time to play.
Cats are plotting on their throne,
While I pretend I'm all alone.

Boredom's knocking on my door,
But I just crank up the snorkel score.
Dancing with a broomstick's flair,
In this corner, nothing's a scare.

The fridge hums a catchy tune,
While I munch a snack, like a raccoon.
Laptop's buzzing with old threads,
While I nap on my own bread.

So here I stay with joy profound,
In comfort's arms, the laughter's found.
Every moment has a twist,
In my cocoon, who could resist?

Enveloping Warmth

A blanket piled, oh what a sight,
Fuzzy slippers, the toes feel right.
Curl up tighter, the world outside,
Might as well be a goofy ride.

Hot cocoa with a marshmallow sail,
As I wade through this warm haze pale.
The cat jumps in, it claims its patch,
We giggle at that furry batch.

Lost my remote, it's made its flight,
Probably hiding from the light.
I'll just use my phone instead,
How did I lose my comfy bed?

So here we bask in laughter's glow,
In this warm nest, no need to show.
Wrapped in joy and silly dreams,
Enveloping warmth, or so it seems.

The Cocoon of Ease

In a chair that swallows me whole,
I lost my plant, or was it a shoal?
Lost in cushions, I'm making waves,
While skipping chores is how one braves.

Out my window, the world can see,
But who cares when there's Netflix spree?
My snack stash bears a telling clue,
Of all the crafting I simply won't do.

Each tiny crease in my soft seat,
Is a journey through snacks oh so sweet.
Remote's on a mission to play hide,
As I dive into comfort's tide.

Cocooned by ease, I stretch and sigh,
Oh look, another nap - oh me, oh my!
This cozy shell makes me believe,
I'm royalty here, with no need to leave!

Echoes of Protection

In this fortress of sock and shoe,
Muffin crumbs are my little glue.
Each echo laughs, a playful sound,
Oh, who knew bliss so tightly bound?

A pillow fort guards my life's throne,
While I crown myself with popcorn's bone.
The walls here whisper secrets sweet,
As a Netflix binge spools on repeat.

Hiding snacks like buried treasure,
Guzzling soda brings me great pleasure.
The couch becomes my kingdom vast,
With every silly show I watch fast.

In echoes soft, I find my bliss,
In this snug life, what could I miss?
With laughter ringing all around,
In this safe space, joy is found.

Serene Horizons

In a bubble of socks and Netflix plays,
Lifeguard of snacks in my daring ways.
The doorbell rings, I hide in my chair,
Is it the pizza guy? Do I even dare?

My couch is my throne, my cat my sage,
Together we plot to escape the cage.
But when the fridge calls, I can't resist,
A dance with leftovers, a gourmet tryst.

When neighbors complain, I don my disguise,
A blanket as robe, and I slowly rise.
"Didn't hear the ruckus, must be your cat,"
As I microwave popcorn, imagining chat.

The windows painted shut with dust and grime,
Each missed social call, a victory chime.
With every pizza, I feel more alive,
In this cozy cocoon, I truly thrive.

Enchanted Domesticity

The laundry folds itself; it's magic, you see,
With clothes on the floor calling out to me.
A vacuum that's shy, it hides from the light,
Avoids all the corners; what a funny sight!

The broom's on vacation, it dreams in a heap,
While I tiptoe past, trying not to creep.
A grocery list written in crayon and flair,
Turns Friday night dinners into a grand affair!

When dishes pile high, I pull out my charm,
A song and a dance to salvage the calm.
The epic battle against crumbs and spills,
Turns into a circus, igniting our thrills!

We bake a cake, flour flies in the air,
It lands on the cat, it's a flour affair.
With giggles and sugar, what more could we need?
Living enchanted inside our home indeed!

The Embrace of Normalcy

In the land of slippers, routines reign supreme,
Coffee in hand, I'm living the dream.
The morning parade of cereal and toast,
Even the burnt bits, I cherish the most!

My hair has its own rebellious spout,
It stands up to greet me; what's that all about?
Mirrors reflect me in all my glory,
A daily adventure, just me and my story.

The plants are my pets, they listen so well,
We gossip and giggle, oh what tales they tell!
They don't judge my outfit — I'm free to be bold,
In my sanctuary, laughter never gets old.

When life seems mundane, I'll throw in some spice,
Dance in my pajamas, oh isn't it nice?
Each normal moment, a canvas so bright,
In the embrace of today, my heart takes flight!

Flourishing in the Familiar

In the cozy chaos of plaid and lace,
Familiarity greets me with a warm embrace.
The fridge hums a tune I know by heart,
From leftovers that feel like culinary art!

My shoes have their own stories to tell,
Old bits of mud, they carry so well.
Each step echoes laughter, memories loud,
In this quirky castle, I stand so proud.

When the doorbell rings with rumors of cheer,
I freeze like a deer, then grin ear to ear.
Banding together, my pals take a stand,
Spinning tales of socks, it's simply unplanned!

The pets roll their eyes at the antics we share,
As we rummage through boxes scattered everywhere.
Yet in this sweet chaos, I bloom and I grow,
Flourishing gracefully in the ebb and flow!

www.ingramcontent.com/pod-product-compliance
Lightning Source LLC
Chambersburg PA
CBHW050307120526
44590CB00016B/2531